1840-1893

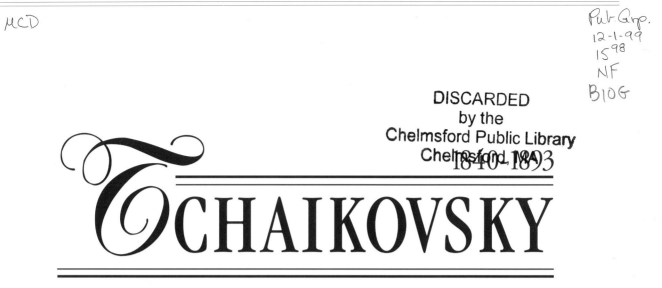

ℭCHAIKOVSKY

1840-1893

TIGER BOOKS INTERNATIONAL
LONDON

© 1995 Bookman International bv
  Houtweg 11, 1251 CR Laren (NH)
  The Netherlands

This book appears under the auspices of Euredition bv, Den Haag,
Netherlands

For this present English language edition: Todtri Productions Ltd.,
New York

Text: Jeroen Koolbergen
Translation: Van Splunteren/Burret
Lay-out: ADM, Pieter van Delft

This edition published in 1995 by Tiger Books International PLC,
Twickenham.

ISBN 1-85501-787-3

Introduction

The Russian composer Igor Stravinsky was responsible for giving fellow countryman Peter Ilyich Tchaikovsky his place in the history of recent Russian music. Stravinksy, a great admirer of Tchaikovsky's, remarked in the 1920s that his music fit the pattern of nineteenth–century development that began with the composer Mikhail Ivanovich Glinka (1804–1857). Glinka was the first to incorporate elements of Russian folk music tinged with nationalism into his operas. His friend and student Alexander Sergeyevich Dargomizhsky worked with texts by the famed Russian poet Pushkin, and he held strong views concerning the relationship between music and text: "I want the sound to express the word." For Stravinsky, Tchaikovsky's music was the logical continuation of these sentiments, even though Tchaikovsky did not belong to the famous Group of Five (the "powerful bunch") of Balakirev, Cui, Rimsky–Korsakov, Borodin, and Moussorgsky. These composers left their mark on Russian music between 1850 and 1900, but were much more nationalistically inclined than Tchaikovsky, who was receptive to German, French, and Italian musical influences.

Tchaikovsky's life was fraught with paradox. Alongside his enormous international musical triumphs were periods of unfulfilled desire and deep depression. No one still knows for sure whether or not the composer committed suicide, though it seems probable, let alone how or why he might have done so.

In any case towards the end of his life Tchaikovsky struggled with a lack of self–confidence (it wasn't until he was forty–seven that he dared to conduct) and his alleged, (repressed) homosexual tendencies.

Tchaikovsky was hugely and bluntly critical of other composers. But he was honest about his own work; he could admit that it was of varying quality.

Much has been saved of his extensive correspondence with his patroness Nadezhda von Meck and the many photographs taken of his contemporaries, intimate friends, and the places where he lived and worked. We will draw heavily on these to follow the life of one of Russia's most renowned composers.

Peter Ilyich Tchaikovsky was born on May 7, 1840 in Kamsko–Votkinsk, a town about 1,000 kilometers (600 miles) east of Moscow. His year of birth took place between premieres of Glinka's two important and innovative operas: *A Life for the Czar* in 1836 and *Russlan and Ludmilla* in 1842.

His father Ilya Petrovich was the director of a factory, earned a prosperous living, and enjoyed high social standing in a city dominated by its metal–working industry. He had been married once before, but had soon become a widower. He had a daughter from this marriage named Zinaida. His second wife, Alexandra Andreyevna d'Assier, whom he married in 1833, bore him six children, the second of whom was Peter Ilyich. His older brother was born in 1838, his sister Alexandra in 1843, brother Ippolit in 1845, and the twins Modest and Anatole in 1850.

The death of his mother in 1854 came as an enormous shock to the fourteen–year–old Peter Ilyich for they had been exceptionally close. He also got on well with the twins and Ippolit, and later his sister and her children would play an important in his life.

The Tchaikovsky family lived at Kamsko–Votkinsk until Peter was about eight years old.

As in many upper–middle–class Russian families, music was an important pastime. He began lessons with a local teacher the moment he showed interest in the piano.

A significant event in his life was the arrival of a Swiss governess. Fanny Dürbach was twenty–two when she came to the family, and it is to her that we owe the following description of just how extraordinarily sensitive young Peter was: "One day Nikolai and Peter could not do a piece of arithmetic, and I really gave them a good talking to, saying how hard their poor father had to work to give them a decent education, etcetera. Nikolai could not have cared less about what I was saying and quickly went on playing as if nothing was wrong. Peter didn't say a word until after supper. And later at bedtime, when I had already forgotten the small incident, he burst out into tears saying how much he loved his parents and how grateful he was to them, reproaching me for having wrongly accused him...In every aspect, his sensitivity knew no bounds, he was a delicate and fragile child."

The governess later recalled that beside the piano, there was an "orchestrion" in the house (a kind of organ that imitated the voices of various instruments), and that as a child Peter had been fascinated by the music that came from both instruments. In a state of half–sleep he could still hear music resounding from them long after the performances in the drawing rooms had ended. They mainly consisted of renditions of Italian and French opera arias done by amateurs. Peter always used to drum along to everything with his fingers, and the story goes he got so excited once he broke a windowpane.

In 1848 Peter's familiar existence came to an end when his father went to Moscow where he thought he would get a better position. But the promises made to him turned out to be bogus, and a year later the family again moved, this time to the provincial city of Alapayevsk, in the vicinity of Nizhni–Novgorod.

In Moscow Peter went to boarding school and took music lessons, and in 1850 at the age of ten, he was registered at the School of Jurisprudence in St. Petersburg. By this time

Top left: *Ilya Petrovich Tchaikovsky, the composer's father.* Right: *His mother Alexandra Andreyevna d'Assier.*

The Tchaikovsky family (Moscow, Glinka Museum). *From left to right: Peter Ilyich, Mother Alexandra, oldest sister Zinaida, Nikolai, Ippolit on his father's knee, and Alexandra (Sasha). The twins had not yet been born. Psychic disorder was a common ailment in Peter's mother's family, the d'Assiers, and Peter inherited this tendency.*

little Peter had several traumatic episodes behind him. First the separation from Fanny Dürbach, to whom he wrote desperate letters from Moscow, and to whom he would continue to write. Then the year at boarding school in his elder sister Zinaida's care and with whom he did not get along. And then, in 1850 he was torn from his mother. He resorted to howling and screaming, and he had to be physically separated from her by force. One can imagine how hard her death hit him four years later. Peter did not merely love her, he worshipped her physical presence.

The Tchaikovsky family house in Kamsko–Votkinsk.

Wolfgang Amadeus Mozart. His opera Don Giovanni *brought Tchaikovsky into transports of rapture at an early age, so much so he later wrote that it made him decide to devote his life to music.*

The shock of her passing was so great it was a year and a half before he could write to Fanny Dürbach. He would never forget the last look on his mother's face after being subjected to the rough–and–ready remedy against cholera, that of submerging the patient in a bath of boiling water.

In St. Petersburg something else happened that would traumatize him yet again. Even though he should have remained in quarantine at school because of a scarlet fever epidemic, Peter went to visit a friend of his father's named Modest Vakar. His son contracted scarlet fever and died. Peter blamed himself for his death.

His childhood impressions of music were extraordinarily intense. He was ecstatic after attending his first ballet performance in 1848. After that his mother took him to see Glinka's opera *A Life for the Czar* in 1849, and in 1850 with Vadar he saw Mozart's *Don Giovanni*. Tchaikovsky described his memories of the latter as follows: "*Don Giovanni* was the first piece of music to totally enthrall me. The effects this transport of rapture caused in me is well known. It gave me the key to the realm of pure beauty, where the greatest geniuses dwell. Until then I had only been exposed to operas by Italian composers. *Don Giovanni* made me decide to devote my entire life to music...In this opera Mozart puts characters on stage who are truly tragic, greater and more impressive than any ever seen in music: Donna Anna...I cannot explain what seizes me when I see this proud, tragic and revengeful beauty appear... When she recognizes Don Giovanni as her father's murderer and her own seducer, when her own rage is released into a masterful recitative and then into a brilliant aria, when pride and fury can be heard in the tiniest chord and tiniest movement of the orchestra, I tremble with awe, I would like to call out, cry, scream it to the rafters."

Below: *A photograph of St. Petersburg at the end of the 19th century. Tchaikovsky was a student at its School for Jurisprudence for nine years.*

Right: *The house the Tchaikovsky family lived in during 1848 and 1849.*

In 1859, after nine years of study at the School of Jurisprudence, Tchaikovsky became a civil servant at the age of nineteen in the Ministry of Justice at St. Petersburg.

His father had moved back to the city in 1852, and so the family had been reunited once again. While a student, Tchaikovsky had been taking piano lessons all along, but no one had the slightest notion he would be able to devote himself wholly to music. Not even his piano instructor Rudolf Küdinger, who stopped his lessons in 1858 because he was not paid and advised him not to pursue a career in music since he "was not highly–gifted enough." Tchaikovsky's father's poor economic status would not improve until his appointment at the age of sixty–three as the director of St. Petersburg's Institute of Technology.

Meanwhile, Peter Ilyich had tried his hand at composing a number of small pieces: a waltz and a chamber music piece based on an Italian text called *Mezzanotte* ("Midnight"). (He had learned a thing or two about the art of singing from a teacher from Naples.) He also wrote a comic opera titled *Hyperbole*.

The young Tchaikovsky was an avid reader. It is a well established fact that he read a great deal of Gogol. But his knowledge of music literature left something to be desired; it appears that not only was he unfamiliar with Beethoven's symphonies, but also the music of Schumann and other significant German composers.

According to the German model, the Union of Russian Music opened a conservatory in St. Petersburg in September 1862. It was set up by the then famous composer and pianist Anton Rubinstein, with Grand Duchess Elena as its patroness. (She was the widow of Czar Paul I's youngest son.) Famous teachers at this conservatory were the Polish violinist Henryk Wieniawski, the cellist Karl Davidov, and the composer Nikolai Zaremba.

In 1861 Tchaikovsky made his first foreign trip; a three month jaunt straight through Europe, including Berlin, Hamburg, Brussels, and Paris. This broadening of his horizons may perhaps have led to his enrollment at the conservatory against the advice of all those around him.

The composer Zaremba took him under his wing, and he began writing his first serious compositions. He supported himself with temporary jobs such as copying music and giving piano lessons. He began work on an opera using Pushkin's famous verse drama *Boris Godunov* as his starting point, but he did not get far. However, he did complete the overture to the famous stage play *The Hurricane* by Alexander Ostrovsky (1823–1886).

In 1865 he wrote music set to Schiller's ode "An die Freude" just as Beethoven had done in his *Ninth Symphony*. It was a good–sized score for chorus and orchestra that was received well by friends and fellow students including the future critic, Hermann Laroche. Official music critics expressed their reservations.

And yet a sign of recognition followed this apparent setback. Anton Rubinstein recommended Tchaikovsky to teach the theory of harmony at the Moscow Conservatory. This conservatory had been set up by Anton's brother Nikolai according to the St. Petersburg model. Tchaikovsky accepted the offer and moved to Moscow in 1866, where he went to live with Nikolai Rubinstein.

Rubinstein was a jovial man who loved good company. He quickly introduced Tchaikovsky to Moscow's intellectual circles, which included such notables as the playwright Ostrovsky and the publisher Jurgenson.

Tchaikovsky began composing his *First Symphony*. It was his first large–scale work. Previously he had composed a piano sonata and a piece for string quartet though neither of them had been published. He had also composed an overture which was favorably received in St. Petersburg. He had been nervous writing the music to Schiller's "Ode to Joy", but Anton Rubinstein had forced him to finish the composition as a kind of conservatory final exam as well as to acquire the teaching certificate in the theory of harmony for Moscow.

Now during the writing of the *First Symphony* he was undergoing a real crisis of nerves that also began to affect his relationship with Nikolai Rubinstein. Tchaikovsky wrote: "I'm on the brink of a nervous breakdown: 1. I cannot go on with the symphony 2. Rubinstein and Tarnovsky have noticed that I'm oversensitive and amuse themselves with needling me 3. I am going to die very soon, before finishing the symphony. I am looking forward to the summer in Kamenka, as if it were the promised land...I hate mankind and would love to retreat to a desert. I have already bought a ticket on the May 10th stage-coach."

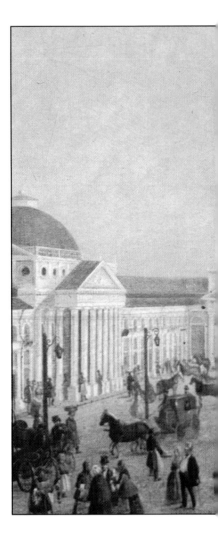

View of Red Square in Moscow, with the church of St. Basil in the middle.

In Kamenka, not far from Kiev, lived Tchaikovsky's sister Alexandra, who was married to Lev Davidov, descendent of a family which had befriended such artists as Pushkin and Gogol. Tchaikovsky would spend the happiest moments of his life on the Davidov's estate.

The First Symphony was received with huge indifference, especially by Peter's friends, even though they knew that composing it had pushed him to the limits of his endurance. Rubinstein conducted the third movement on December 26, 1866 in Moscow. However, a complete performance did not take place until 1868.

*Anton (left) and Nikolai
Rubinstein. Nikolai was also a
pianist. Tchaikovsky composed the
Russian Scherzo for him.*

The symphony's subtitle is "Winter Dreams" and it includes similar captions to each section, such as "Travel Dreams" and "Landscape in Fog." Tchaikovsky follows in Glinka's footsteps particularly during the Scherzo and Finale, when like him, he is able to integrate Russian folk music into the most developed art of composition.

Tchaikovsky himself wrote that he was carried away by his fascination for the countryside: "A simple Russian landscape, an evening walk in summer, across the land, through the forest or over the steppes makes me so emotional that I stretch myself out on the ground, seized by a

silent paralysis, by an overwhelming feeling for nature, totally upset by the dizzying scene all around me, by the forest, by the steppes, by the river, by the village in the distance, by the simple country church, by everything that is part of the scenery of my native land, Russia."

Nevertheless, Tchaikovsky proved himself not to be a slave to the rigidly academic methods taught by Zaremba at the St. Petersburg Conservatory: "For certain compositions, such as the symphony, the form is pre–determined, and I adhere to it. But only as far as the major outlines are concerned, and the order of the sections. I believe great liberties may be taken with

the details, as long as they are the consequence of a natural development of a musical idea."

In 1866 Tchaikovsky also composed an occasional piece, an overture that quotes the Danish national anthem, in honor of the marriage of the heir apparent to the throne, the czarevitch (the future Czar Alexander III) with Princess Dagmar of Denmark. The following year he dedicated himself to an even bigger project: an opera with a libretto by Ostrovsky, based on his own play *The Dream of the Volga*. The work on this opera progressed badly owing to Ostrovsky's slowness. In the end, the opera was a dismal flop and in February 1869 after only five perfor-

mances Tchaikovsky tore the score to shreds in Moscow. In the meantime he had composed a piano piece for Rubinstein entitled the *Russian Scherzo*. Tchaikovsky had also returned to Moscow from his vacation at his sister's in Kamenka in 1867 with three piano compositions: *Ruins of a Castle, Scherzo,* and *Song Without Words*, collected under the title *Memories of Hapsal*. (Hapsal is the harbor on the Baltic Sea where Peter and his brother Modest traveled on their way to Kamenka.)

Tchaikovsky's favorite sister Alexandra, with her husband Lev Davidov, around 1860. The couple lived in a large house in Kamenka, not far from Kiev, in the Ukraine. Tchaikovsky came here often and really enjoyed taking part in family life, fond as he was of his sister's children.

During the same period when Tchaikovsky's opera The Voyevode was poorly received, the composer made the acquaintance of colleagues and contemporaries who called themselves "The Five." The leader of this nationalist company, Mily Alexandrovich Balakirev (1837–1910) (top) would influence him greatly. Tchaikovsky had him to thank for the idea of writing a symphonic poem based on Shakespeare's play Romeo and Juliet. The other members of "The Five" were Alexander Borodin (1833–1887), Cesar Antonovitch Cui (1835–1918), Modest Moussorsky (1839–1881), and Nikolai Rimsky–Korsakov (1844–1908). Although Tchaikovsky agreed in broad terms with their nationalistic views, he was not very convinced about the quality of their music.

Score cover of the symphonic poem Romeo & Juliet. This edition was published by the prestigious Berlin publishingh house Bote & Bock (Milan, Library of the Verdi Conservatory). Romeo & Juliet was Tchaikovsky's first big masterpiece and became a success throughout Europe, even though it had been coolly received at first (in March 1869, in Moscow).

The French singer Desirée Artôt made such an impression on Tchaikovsky he fancied he had fallen in love with her. The feeling was not mutual.

Ever since he was a little child, Tchaikovsky had been fascinated by the women in his immediate surroundings. First his mother and then his governess Fanny Dürbach and later his sister–in–law, Vera Davidova. But by now it was clear to the composer that he was homosexual, like his brother Modest, to whom he had confided this. Modest would always act as his protector, so much so that essential information about Tchaikovsky's friendships and how he met his own end, have always remained in the dark. Modest cannot really be blamed for this because in czarist Russia, homosexuality was certainly not *bon ton.*

It is certain that Tchaikovsky had a number of friends since coming to live in Moscow, even though the precise nature of these relationships is not clear. Among these were two brothers, Vladimir and Konstantin Shilovsky. Vladimir accompanied the composer on his trips. Tchaikovsky was also fond of his nephew Vladimir Davidov, called "Bob" for short, with whom he remained close to his dying day.

Nevertheless, Tchaikovsky let it be known to everyone he greatly appreciated the company of women and that someday he wished to get married. This was probably a combination of the necessity to mislead the outside world, and a real, if somewhat naive desire to live together with a woman, that stemmed from his intense memories of the women from his childhood.

Having reached this stage in his life, in 1868 he met the French singer Desirée Artôt, who had performed in Moscow's Bolshoi Theater. Tchaikovsky the musician was especially interested in the French woman, and he even followed her to Paris. He wrote enthusiastically to his brother Modest: "What a singer! What an actress! No actor has ever made such an impression on me, and how sorry I am that you cannot see and hear her! You would be thrilled with her gestures and the boundless elegance of her movements. ...I have become very good friends with her and she is very sweet to me. ...Seldom have I seen such a lovable, forthright, and intelligent woman."

Photograph of Tchaikovsky with a fragment from the "Andante cantabile" from the First String Quartet *(1871).*

Portrait of Desirée Artôt, at age 22. Tchaikovsky's infatuation with her presumably sprang from his need and obligation to convince the world that he was indeed "normal."

Tchaikovsky clearly misread the situation for shortly thereafter Desirée Artôt married the Spanish baritone, Mariano Padilla y Ramos. A later affair would lead to both marriage and a real drama.

For Tchaikovsky the 1870s were very productive musically and he traveled extensively throughout Europe. The works written in this period include the *First String Quartet, Six Romances* (for piano and voice), the opera *Undine*, the *Second Symphony*, the opera *The Oprichnik* (The Royal Bodyguard), the symphonic fantasy *The Tempest* based on Shakespeare's play, the *Second String Quartet*, and the opera *Vakula the Blacksmith*. (This last piece being reworked in 1885 into *The Mules*.) It was the time in which Moussorgsky was working on his *Boris Godunov* and Rimsky–Korsakov on The *Girl from Pskov*. The members of the Group of Five could be satisfied with the nationalistic

Top left: *The pianist, composer, and conductor Hans von Bülow, was the great champion of Tchaikovsky's* First Piano Concerto.

Top right: *The title page of his first publication.*

*Portrait of Sergei Taneyev
(1856–1915), pianist, composer,
and critic who performed
Tchaikovsky's First Piano
Concerto to great acclaim in
Moscow. They remained lifelong
friends.*

Hans von Bülow conducting the First Piano Concerto.

ideas Tchaikovsky had woven into his opera *The Opritchnik*, which takes place during the reign of Czar Ivan the Terrible, and in the *Second Symphony* with the subtitle "The Little Russian."

By the end of December 1873, Tchaikovsky left the house he had been sharing with Nikolai Rubinstein. He now lived in a house with Sofronov, a personal servant and jack–of–all–trades, whose presence meant a great deal to the composer. It was in this house that Tchaikovsky completed his *Concerto for Piano and Orchestra No. 1* at the end of 1874. He hastened to submit it to Nikolai Rubinstein, who was just as famous a pianist as his brother Anton. Rubinstein's reaction was so negative the composer took away his dedication to Rubinstein, dedicating the concerto to the renowned pianist and conductor Hans von Bülow, who promptly put it on his program throughout Europe and the United States, espe-

cially in Boston and New York. After a mediocre première with a bad pianist and conductor in St. Petersburg, the concerto was well received in Moscow. The solo passages were played by one of Tchaikovsky's students, the composer and conductor Sergei Taneyev. Some time later Rubinstein admitted his mistake, and even included it in his repertoire. Tchaikovsky himself revised the score fifteen years later. This version is the one now performed by every major pianist in the world.

The towers of the Kremlin as seen from across the Moscow River in a print, circa 1840.

Portrait of Tchaikovsky in 1875. With the dedication: "For Nikolai Andreyevich Rimsky–Korsakov, in sincerest friendship –Moscow May 18, 1875."

Tchaikovsky finished his *Third Symphony* while staying with his sister in Kamenka. It was first performed in November 1875. This symphony was called the "Polish" because the finale employs the rhythm of the Polish dance, the *polonaise*. The symphony is unorthodox in structure, having five instead of the usual four-movements, and the music alternates between sounding like a series of dances and a proper symphony. A famous previous example of a similar blend of styles is Berlioz's *Symphonie fantastique*.

The great French composer Camille Saint–Saëns attended the opening night of Tchaikovsky's *Third Symphony*. Tchaikovsky, who closely followed French cultural developments dearly wanted to befriend Saint–Saëns who was not only a composer, but an excellent pianist and conductor and at the forefront of innovations in French music. They discovered

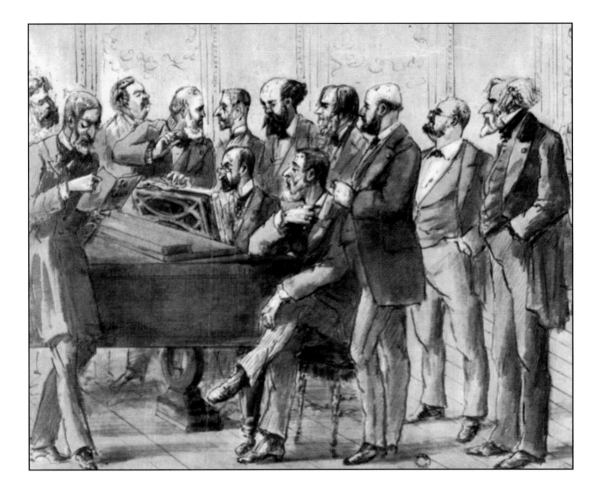

A gathering of composers in Paris (Paris, Musée Carnavalet). Tchaikovsky's friend Saint–Saëns seated at the piano, Charles Gounod with his hand resting on his knee, César Franck with his characteristically long sideburns behind Saint–Saëns, and Ambroise Thomas, to the far right.

that, among other things, they shared a passion for ballet which caused a curious scene in the great rehearsal hall at the Moscow Conservatory. With Nikolai Rubinstein improvising at the piano to music from the ballet *Galatea and Pygmalion*, Tchaikovsky and Saint–Saëns performed a *pas de deux*, with Tchaikovsky as Pygmalion and the bearded Saint–Saëns, then in his forties, as Galatea.

The friendship between the two composers was sealed when Tchaikovsky visited Paris in 1876. It was here that he finished the greater part of the music for *Swan Lake*, which he had been commissioned to compose. Its première at the Bolshoi Theater in 1877 went practically unnoticed. It was not until 1895, two years after his death that the ballet became a huge success, choreographed by Marius Petipa (1822–1910).

In Paris Tchaikovsky discovered Bizet's masterpiece *Carmen*, a few months after the composer's death. He was immediately convinced of its worth: "No one is a prophet in his own country; the Parisians were not able to understand *Carmen*; but I'm utterly convinced that in ten years this will be the most popular opera in the world." As far as his appreciation is concerned he found himself in rather heterogeneous company; other admirers included Bismarck and Johannes Brahms, not to mention Friedrich Nietzsche, who united all anti–Wagnerians under *Carmen*'s banner.

In 1876 Tchaikovsky signed a contract with a Russian magazine to compose a piano piece once a month, inspired by that month. His servant Sofronov had to remind him at the beginning of each month. The composition was then finished in two days. (They have been collected as *The Seasons, Opus 37b*.) He further took it upon himself to cover the ceremonial opening of the Wagner festival in Bayreuth for a Russian

Handwritten mss. of Swan Lake
*(Berlin, Bildarchiv Preussischer
Kulturbesitz).*

29

Interior of Moscow's Bolshoi Theater where on March 4, 1877 the first performance of Swan Lake *took place without much success.*

newspaper. He wrote a lively chronicle about it, that left Wagner and Bayreuth in tatters. He was friendly enough with Liszt and Wagner, but would not budge in his judgment of their music: "The music (Liszt's) leaves me cold; it's more like a poem in color than a real creation; it's a painting without a subject. Everything he composes is dazzling, but with no structure whatsoever. What a difference with Schumann whose enormous creative powers were not in relation to the means with which he wished to express them." About Wagner: "Upon hearing the final chords of the *Twilight of the Gods* I felt as though I had been freed from prison. I know for certain that no one has ever composed anything that is longer, with less power and more boring than the Nibelungen cycle... Music was once

Tchaikovsky in 1877, when he had resolved to marry "whoever I wish to," because "our inclinations are our greatest and most insurmountable obstacles to achieving happiness, and we must fight with all our might against our nature..." as he wrote to his brother Modest.

Wedding portrait of Peter Ilyich
Tchaikovsky and Antonina
Milyukova, July 18, 1877.

The Kremlin and the Moscow River (Berlin, Archiv für Kunst und Geschichte).

meant to afford pleasure to its listeners; with Wagner it's torture and a marathon that ends in exhaustion."

In the meantime Tchaikovsky had published his *Third String Quartet*, the *March Slav*, the *Rococo Variations* for cello and orchestra, and the symphonic fantasy *Francesca da Rimini*, which he had been inspired to write by reading Dante in the train between Vichy and Bayreuth. At the beginning of the score he wrote: "Lament the past, hope for the future, never be satisfied with the present, that is what makes up my life."

Tchaikovsky was now thirty–seven years old, an established composer, but an extremely neurotic personality. He sought relief by writing letters, sometimes eighteen a day. His friend Laroche, for example, received over four thousand.

It was around this time that rumors of his supposed homosexuality began circulating so widely he deemed counter measures were in order. It had already cost him a great deal of money to nip potential scandals in the bud. He now decided that a marriage was the best way to put the rumors to rest once and for all. As chance would have it he had received a number of fiery love letters during this period from a twenty–eight–year–old woman by the name of Antonina Milyukova. He resolved to take her up on her advances. They were engaged and married shortly thereafter on July 18, 1877. Little did he know that Antonina was a schemer and to top it all off, stupid, snobbish, and a nymphomaniac. She had written love letters to everybody in the capital who was anybody, including numerous members of the czar's family. Three days after their marriage Tchaikovsky wrote a desperate letter to his brother Anatole: "It would have been unforgivable of me had I misled my

33

Tchaikovsky (right) and his former pupil, the violinist Josef Kotek. The composer was sexually attracted to him, though this interest was probably not mutual, owing to Kotek's great love for the female of the species.

wife, had I not warned her that she could only count on brotherly love. Physically she fills me with utter disgust."

Nevertheless the couple went on a short honeymoon, but once back in Moscow the composer fled to Kamenka, on the pretext that he was going to the Caucasus for a cure. Naturally he had to return to Moscow after a while, but he despaired so much of his wife's pushiness that on an evening in October he walked into the ice cold waters of the Moscow River in hopes of becoming seriously ill. When this failed he asked his brother Anatole in St. Petersburg to send a telegram with a supposed invitation from the orchestra director, Napravnik. Anatole picked up his brother, on the brink of nervous exhaustion, at the train station and he and Nikolai Rubinstein decided to intervene. They visited Antonina, who turned out to be stupider than they feared, to try and get her to divorce Tchaikovsky. She refused and continued to do so, even after she had given birth to two illegitimate children. Finally, after years of following Tchaikovsky around and blackmailing him with her knowledge of his sexual preference, she agreed to live in Odessa, a long way from where her husband resided. Because Tchaikovsky took

pity on her increasingly unstable mental condition he left the matter at that. Antonina Milyukova would spend the last twenty years of her life in a mental institution.

His marriage had put the rumors of his homosexuality to rest, for a while that is. Tchaikovsky's brothers Anatole and Modest had taken him from St. Petersburg to Clarens in Switzerland where he stayed in the pension Villa Richelieu. Beginning in October 1877 he spent seven months abroad, with trips to Florence, Vienna, and Paris.

Just before his marriage, a former student of Tchaikovsky's had put him in touch with the widow Nadezhda von Meck. Her husband had made a fortune in real estate and by laying the

Nadezhdā von Meck, Tchaikovsky's patroness from 1877 onward. The composer reveals more about himself in his correspondence with her than with anyone else.

Page of a letter Tchaikovsky wrote to Nadezhda von Meck, nine days after his marriage in July 1877. He asked her for money, to go on a cure in the Caucasus, far from his wife. Von Meck sent 1,000 roubles, but Tchaikovsky went to his sister and brother–in–law in Kamenka.

first two Russian railroads. Besides leaving her a fortune, he also left her with twelve children to raise. Nadezhda von Meck had hated marriage as an institution, and now she threw herself into acting as patron and protector to promising and famous musicians, which she did for awhile for Claude Debussy. She was ugly, authoritarian, and a hypochondriac. She thought of Tchaikovsky as a kind of court musician to whom she gave commissions. All contact was carried on through correspondence (their collected letters run to three volumes), and they never met in person although Tchaikovsky did stay at her "Brailov" estate a few times.

Even though Nadezhda von Meck might have been jealous, she had no objections to Tchaikovsky's marriage. Presumably, she was unaware of his homosexuality for quite some time. Her stream of commissions made Tchaikovsky financially independent but in exchange he had to show her unconditional obedience in a practically feudal way.

To get away from his wife, Tchaikovsky traveled in October 1877 with his brothers Anatole and Modest to Clarens, Switzerland and then on to Italy. Top: Tchaikovsky (right) with his brother Modest in San Remo in 1878. Standing: Alexei Sofronov, Tchaikovsky's personal servant, whom he depended on more and more, and to the left little "Kolya," a deaf and dumb student of Modest's.

The libretto of Eugene Onegin, *Tchaikovsky's most important opera, was based on the novel of the same name by Alexander Pushkin (right). The opera was first performed in Moscow in March 1879. Above a scene from this first performance where Onegin and Lensky quarrel during Tatiana's birthday party (Act II).*

Nadezhda von Meck's Brailova estate. Tchaikovsky stayed in the main building only when Madame von Meck was not there. Otherwise he stayed in an old country manor elsewhere on the estate. The composer and his nine–year–senior admirer had made an agreement they would never meet. If they happened to be at a concert or elsewhere they acted as if they did not know each other. This strange order of business predominately had to do with Nadezhda von Meck's neurotic need for privacy. She usually traveled in her own private train and was only socially active with her family and servants.

During Tchaikovsky's foreign sojourn in 1877–1878 three major compositions occupied his time: the *Fourth Symphony*, the opera *Eugene Onegin*, which he had blocked out prior to his marriage, and the *Concerto for Violin and Orchestra in D major*, which was conceived in Clarens. Also dating from this period is the *Sonata for Piano in G major, Opus 37*. It was dedicated to the then famous pianist, Karl Klindworth (1830–1916), but quickly vanished from the repertoire.

The libretto for the opera *Eugene Onegin* was

based on a novel by Pushkin, and deals with the love lives of members of the Russian upper middle class in the 1830s. The plot is simple. Tatiana writes a love letter to Onegin who politely refuses her. To annoy his friend Lensky, Onegin begins courting his fiancée, Olga, who is Tatiana's sister. This leads to a quarrel which ends in a duel between Onegin and Lensky in which the latter is killed. Years later Onegin meets Tatiana and falls in love with her, but it is too late for she is now married to the Prince Gremin. She decides to remain true to her husband even though she admits she still loves Onegin.

Vladimir (Bob) Davidov, Tchaikovsky's favorite nephew, for whom he wrote his Child's Album, *during a stay at Madame von Meck's Brailov estate in 1878. Bob was then seven years old.*

The première took place in 1879 at the Imperial Music College in Moscow for a mainly invited audience, and then officially in 1881, again in Moscow. It is understandable why the opera was not a success at first. It was not composed in the traditional style of Italian and French repertoire opera nor in the nationalistic mode of Tchaikovsky's contemporaries. Tchaikovsky's aversion to Wagner's musical dramatic style was clearly evident, and the sum total of this made it practically incomprehensible to the Russian public. But as far as this composition was concerned, Tchaikovsky was completely convinced of himself: "the artist should not allow himself to be influenced by the blindness of his contemporaries. He must find ways to express that which is in him, that needs to be said. Only time will measure the value of his work, and if I am now able to face criticism with courage, it is because I have an irrepressible faith in the future. I can already taste and am enjoying the little bit of fame that will befall me in the history of Russian music."

Czar Alexander II of Russia, who ruled from 1855 to 1881. After the dictatorial reign of his father Nicolas I, he pushed through important reforms such as the abolition of serfdom in 1861. He was killed in a bomb attack in 1881.

The coronation of Alexander II in 1855, the year in which Russia lost the Crimean War. (Berlin, Bildarchiv Preussischer Kulturbesitz).

Some of Tchaikovsky's friends did like *Eugene Onegin*, but not his *Concerto for Violin and Orchestra*. The piece was dedicated to Leopold Auer, but was first played by Adolf Brodsky in Vienna in 1881. Tchaikovsky had been inspired by Edouard Lalò's *Spanish Symphony* (a violin concerto despite its name), which he himself had conducted often with Josef Kotek playing the violin. Tchaikovsky's violin concerto was pan-

Back from his foreign journey, after the marriage crisis, Tchaikovsky went to live with his sister in Kamenka for a while. Here he wrote the short pieces such as *Child's Album* and *March of the Fleet Volunteers*. The latter inspired by Czar Alexander II's victory against the Ottoman Empire during the war of 1877–1878. This victory and the annexation of the Caucasus and large tracts of Central Asia were then partly annulled by the intervention of British and Austrian diplomats at the Congress of Berlin in 1878.

A strange work also arose in Kamenka: the *Liturgy of St. John Chrysostom*. Tchaikovsky was not an especially religious man. As he wrote to Nadezhda von Meck: "as far as religion is concerned I must confess I possess confused ideas and have not been successful in resolving all manner of contradictions. ... Without music I would go crazy...Solely through the love of music is our life worth living, and let us profit from it richly before we are laid out in the earth." Yet Tchaikovsky was sensitive to the attractions liturgy held, just as other Russian composers such as Sergei Rachmaninov who wrote beautiful vespers, and Igor Stravinsky. Tchaikovsky often went to church in Kamenka. "In my opinion, the liturgy of St. John Chrysostom is one of the most fascinating artistic creations that exists," he wrote. "And I also love the vespers, on Saturday, in an old chapel. There you remain seated in the half darkness, surrounded by the odor of incense asking yourself the familiar things: why, when, where, where to?...But the choir starts singing and you surrender to the enchantment."

The Liturgy of St. John Chrysostom was performed to great acclaim in St. Petersburg in December 1880. But the clergy objected and the religious authorities raised their voice in protest: "It is about the liturgy of St. John Chrysostom, but the program notes say it's by P.I. Tchaikovsky! Sacred music belongs to the church and not to concert halls. The liturgical text is not some little fable to be used to slap together some libretto!"

ned by the leading German critic Eduard Hanslick, who was normally so unbiased and cautious. But his review spoke of a "stench" rising from the composition. No doubt this prejudiced view had to do with the independent stance the French and the Russians took when it came to traditional German music. Berlioz and Glinka are examples of this.

Still on the run from his wife, Tchaikovsky left Kamenka for Nadezhda von Meck's Brailov estate where he stayed for a while before proceeding to Florence where she had found him a house near her villa. Here he worked on an idea for an opera about Joan of Arc, *The Maid of Orléans* using Schiller's tragedy as his starting point.

Then he traveled to Paris, attending a concert of his own *The Tempest*, which the audience booed. Then he went on to St. Petersburg for the première of *Eugene Onegin*. At Brailov he continued work on *The Maid of Orléans*, and in December 1879 he returned to Italy, this time to discover the beauty of Rome. "I tarried long in the Sistine Chapel and a miracle took place there: for the first time in my life a painting truly elicited excitement in me as an artist." Tchaikovsky paid homage to the Eternal City with the colorful piece of music entitled *Capriccio Italien*. It is descriptive and picturesque in style; for instance it uses cavalry fanfares that accompanied the King of Italy's guard. The composer heard them pass under his window every evening.

Tchaikovsky also returned home with a rough sketch for the *Second Concerto for Piano and Orchestra in G major*. This piece has always had less success than the first piano concerto, maybe because, despite its typically Tchaikovsky style, it has fewer moments of grandeur.

Back in Moscow in 1880, Tchaikovsky could see that he was at the height of his fame. His compositions were on every poster in all the concert halls of Europe and the United States, and audiences in the capital and major cities began clamoring for his presence. Performances of his operas followed quickly on each other's heels and *The Maid of Orléans* won back those fans who had left after *Eugene Onegin*. The reason was simple: the historical tale of Joan of Arc, produced in an operatic style that was

currently popular, was an enormous hit. His first sketches for the opera *Mazeppa* based on Pushkin's poem *Poltava* continued in this vein.

Financially speaking things were going well for Tchaikovsky and he was less dependent on Nadezhda von Meck. He could no longer stay at Kamenka, however, because his sister Alexandra was seriously ill. That is why he bought a country house in Maidanova near Klin, where he lived when he did not have to be in Moscow or travel. This house is now the Tchaikovsky Museum. He put a sign on his door that said he would only receive visitors on Thursdays from three to five in the afternoon and that no one should ring the doorbell.

Tchaikovsky's fame led to his being taken under the protection of the imperial family, most notably by Czarina Maria Feodorovna and Grand Duke Konstantin. Every now and then he had composed an occasional piece such as the 1812 *Overture*, to inaugurate the Cathedral of Christ the Savior. He called this overture " a lot of noise about nothing." As far as noise was concerned he was right since he added booming cannonfire to evoke Napoleon's retreat from Russia. However, he was very satisfied with another composition from the same period, the *Serenade in C major, Opus* 48. This suite, written in an eighteenth–century style, was done so "of inner necessity."

From now on he was commissioned to compose more music for the imperial family. In 1881 Czar Alexander II was murdered, and shortly thereafter came the coronation of his successor, Alexander III. On this occasion the composer was commissioned to write a *Solemn March*, and a vocal work that was entitled, *Moscow*. It took him six weeks of continuous work, and he was rewarded with a ring set with a diamond worth 1,500 roubles. Yet he would rather have received cash, for after he hocked the ring for 375 roubles, he lost the pawn ticket.

Tchaikovsky's country home and garden in Klin.

*A corner of the bedroom in the
country house in Klin.
(Now the Tchaikovsky Museum).*

*Czar Alexander III, who ascended
to the throne after the murder of
his father in 1881.*

At the end of March 1880 Tchaikovsky was in Nice when a telegram arrived with the news that Nikolai Rubinstein had died in Paris. This tragic event later inspired him to write the *Trio in A minor, Opus 50*, for piano, violin, and cello. He rushed off to Paris where he found his friend's body lying in state in the Russian church in Rue Daru. Rubinstein had been an important person in Tchaikovsky's life, and the composer was just as upset as he had been at the loss of his mother. Rubinstein remained as headstrong as ever, right up to his death. When he knew his health had been ruined by tuberculosis of the intestines, he purposely ate a forbidden meal of oysters. It killed him three hours later.

The years 1881 to 1885 were not particularly fruitful ones for Tchaikovsky, despite the publi-

The exorbitantly ornate coronation of Czar Alexander III who reigned from 1881 to 1894. A royal march by Tchaikovsky was played, which he had had two weeks to compose.

Tchaikovsky in a photograph in 1879.

cation of a few important works such as *The Maid of Orléans, Mazeppa*, two suites for orchestra, and the *Concert Fantasy for Piano and Orchestra*, along with less important compositions including the cycle *Sixteen Songs for Young People*.

This less than satisfying period ended with the composition of the symphonic poem *Manfred*, inspired by the well–known poem by Byron, and more or less foisted upon him by the composer Balakirev, who deemed the subject unsuitable for himself but all good material for Tchaikovsky. He worked hard on it during the summer of 1885, using Berlioz's *Symphonie fantastique* as his model. The result was a work of gigantic proportions, but whose every detail was finely wrought. Balakirev conducted its opening per-

Tchaikovsky's loyal personal valet
Alexei Sofronov with his wife.
Sofronov increasingly took care of
the composer's day–to–day wor-
ries, who completely left everything to him. Alexei was twenty
years younger than his employer,
having succeeded his older brother. He was a stabilizing factor in
Tchaikovsky's life. He dined with
him and accompanied the composer on walks and to the theater.
Tchaikovsky loved him without a
physical relationship ever deve-
loping. He used his influence to
reduce Sofronov's mandatory
six–year military service to half
that amount.

formance in St. Petersburg in 1886, and it was
enthusiastically received, even by the composer
and critic Cui, who had never been a great fan
of Tchaikovsky's before.1886 saw the composer
alternately on the road or at home in Klin. He
visited his brother Ippolit who was in the navy,
and whose ship lay at anchor in the Sea of Azov,
then his other brother Anatole, who had settled
in Tiflis. Then he traveled by sea to
Constantinople and Marseille and from there to
Paris. By this time he was a star in the French
capital and moved in fashionable circles. He was

thus able to meet many composers, such as Delibes and the young Fauré. He was also received in the salon of the famous singer Pauline Viardot, who had had a relationship with the Russian writer Turgenev. It was here he was shown Mozart's handwritten score of *Don Giovanni*, an emotional event for the man who had dedicated his life to music because of this opera....

He was working on a new opera in this period called *The Sorceress* based on a play by a contemporary writer, Ippolit Shapazhinsky. Tchaikovsky himself conducted its opening performance on November 1, 1887 at the Maryinsky Theater in St. Petersburg, recalling it as a "downright fiasco."

In the spring of 1887 he again made a long journey through Russia, traveling on the Volga. He studied the score of *Don Giovanni*, and as a sort of homage to his favorite composer, he wrote the *Fourth Suite for Orchestra*, nicknamed "Mozartiana" because in each section musical motifs from Mozart's work can be heard.

After the fiasco of *The Sorceress*, Tchaikovsky again went abroad, this time directly through Europe. He spent Christmas in Leipzig, at the home of the violinist Brodsky, who had been the first to play his violin concerto. He met Johannes Brahms and Edvard Grieg, though he preferred the Norwegian composer to the great German master who "was rather fond of the bottle." (A nasty remark that Tchaikovsky, himself a big drinker, had no right making.) His journey continued on to Berlin where he saw his "childhood sweetheart," Desirée Artôt, and heard the first symphony by a young composer named Richard Strauss. In Prague he became friends with Antonin Dvorák. Then he went to

Paris and London, where he conducted for the first time, just as he had done in Leipzig.

During this concert tour and on into 1889 and 1890 he was working on three entirely different scores: The *Fifth Symphony*, the ballet *The Sleeping Beauty*, and the opera *The Queen of Spades*. He conducted the symphony's first performance in November 1888. The overture that he wrote at about the same time, *Hamlet*, was a commission from a Parisian actor who needed a piece of music for Shakespeare's drama. The composer Balakirev was not too fond of it, judging by the remark he wrote in the score during the love theme of Hamlet and Ophelia: "Hamlet shows his respect for Ophelia by offering her an ice cream."

The Gewandhaus in Leipzig. Tchaikovsky made his debut there as a conductor in 1888. His new career as conductor would never prove financially lucrative.

*The old concert building in
Hamburg, where Tchaikovsky
conducted during his second tour
as a conductor in 1889.*

Towards the end of 1890 a sha-
dow fell over Tchaikovsky's suc-
cesses. Nadezhda von Meck
(right), his patroness at a distance,
severed all connections with him.
Her financial situation had deteri-
orated, and after thirteen years she
cut off Tchaikovsky's annual
allowance. (Owing to the fact he
received an annual salary from
Alexander III this was not a disas-
ter; besides his income had risen
sharply due to success both at
home and abroad.) However, there
was more behind this radical step.
Members of her family were perhaps afraid Tchaikovsky would
receive part of the inheritance.
And other musicians who received
her patronage, convinced her that
Tchaikovsky was not worth her
attention; worse than that they fill-
ed her in on his homosexual pro-
clivities, which were no longer a
secret in musical circles in Russia
or abroad. In a letter sent on
October 4, 1890 to announce her
intention to break with him, she
banally announced: "Do not forget me and think about me from
time to time." Tchaikovsky, who
again lost a mother figure, felt
betrayed and never forgave her.
They would never hear from each
other again, and Nadezhda von
Meck died a few weeks after
Tchaikovsky in 1893.

The Royal Opera in Berlin where Tchaikovsky's music was especially well received by the critics.

The ballet *The Sleeping Beauty* was also a commission from the renowned choreographer Marius Petipa (who would produce a successful version of *Swan Lake* in 1895). It was based on the fable by Perrault. There was a preview for Czar Alexander III, and the first public performance took place on January 15, 1890.

Afterwards Tchaikovsky worked on a new opera with a libretto by his brother Modest, *The Queen of Spades*, based on a story by Pushkin. After a difficult start the composer became taken with his subject, and he finished the score between June and September so that the première could take place on December 19, 1890. The man who commissioned the opera, the director of St. Petersburg's Maryinsky Theater, expected a score along the lines of Bizet's recent success, *Carmen*. What he got was something altogether different. *The Queen of Spades*, just like *Eugene Onegin*, is based on a personal lyricism that does justice to all levels of expression, from intimacy to intense realism. In this regard these two operas had more in common with Verdi's last operas, *Otello* and *Falstaff*, and Puccini's first operas, *Manon Lescaut* and *La Boheme*, while the natural style of singing does not go as far as the verism of Leoncavallo (*Pagliacci*) and Mascagni (*Cavalleria Rusticana*). The opera opened in December 1890 at St. Petersburg's Maryinsky Theater and was an immediate smash success.

Tchaikovsky almost always had a notebook with him to jot down musical ideas. This page contains commentary and thoughts concerning the opera The Queen of Spades, *which occupied him in 1889.*

Title page of a Moscow publication of the opera The Queen of Spades *(Milan, Library of the Verdi Conservatory). Behind the queen of spades we see the three cards of fate: the three of clubs, seven of diamonds, and ace of spades.*

Tchaikovsky with the young pian-
ist Alexander Ziloty (1863–1945)
one of the young musicians he
befriended at an older age. Ziloty
gave him some advice in making
certain revisions for the First
Piano Concerto.

The Tchaikovsky brothers circa 1890. From left to right: Anatole, Nikolai, Ippolit, Peter Ilyich, and Modest. Their sister Alexandra (Sasha) who had been long ill, died in April 1891 when Tchaikovsky was in France on his way to the United States.

Tchaikovsky on the Art of Composing

In letters to his patroness Nadezhda von Meck dated July 6 and 7, 1878 he responds to her question about how he approached the art of composition.

My dear friend, this is a delicate question, owing to the fact each new work arises under different circumstances. I shall try nonetheless to explain to you how it happens in general terms; to explain to you my methods it is first of all necessary to divide my compositions into two categories: those which I have written for myself brought on by a sudden unexpected brainwave or from some inner necessity; and the kind that is inspired by events in the outside world, or for which I have received a commission, such as the cantata for the Polytechnic Exhibition or the "March Sláv" for the Red Cross concert. I must hasten to add that the quality of a composition is in no way dependent on which category is involved. A commissioned piece can often turn out excellent, while the fruit of personal and spontaneous inspiration can succeed less because of various unforeseen circumstances. In fact the circumstances in which the composer found himself at the time while he was working are of the utmost importance, and that determines his entire frame of mind. When the composer is in the process of creation he should be totally at ease. In this respect a work of art is always "objective" even when it comes to music...

You cannot summon the will for compositions in the first category. You have to obey an inner voice and if outside forces do not hinder the act of creation then the composition will progress with utmost ease. You are oblivious to everything around you and time flies with out being noticed. It is akin to sleepwalking: you are unaware of being alive. It is impossible to describe such moments: when it happens as such everything that flows from your pen, either as a sketch or as a project in your mind, is of great value; if the outside world does not disturb the artist, he will create a masterpiece.

For compositions written as commissioned pieces you sometimes have to force inspiration along. First, you often have to get over your initial laziness or lack of enthusiasm in order to get down to work. At that moment obstacles arise. One day you overcome them with ease, the next day your inspiration dries up without the slightest hope of it ever returning! Yet the artist must never give up. You cannot afford to sit and wait for inspiration to come: inspiration does not come to the lazy but to those who summon her.

We Russians are accused of not being dynamic or creative souls; this accusation is correct insofar as the Russian is lazy by nature. He loves to put off until tomorrow what he can do today; he has great natural born talents, but by nature he is not master of himself. That is something you have to achieve: we have to learn to be masters of ourselves and not give way to the amateurism that attaches itself even to the great Glinka. While he was creative by nature and lived to be a ripe old age he has only left a few works for posterity. Read his memoirs and you will see he

only composed when he felt like it, for his pleasure, as an amateur. ...

Dear friend, I hope inspiration will not accuse me of arrogance when I tell you that I never call her in vain. For quite some time now, she whom I consider to be an unpredictable visitor, has gotten used to me; we have become inseparable; she only leaves me when she feels she is unnecessary because my human existence and daily life have disturbed us.

But this little cloud soon passes, and my visitor returns. I can truly say I compose music everywhere, at every moment of the day. It amuses me that I am sometimes visited by inspiration while I am standing and talking to people who have nothing to do with music. A kind of mechanism is triggered in my brain, in the music department of my powers of thought. Sometimes it is a simple melodic detail, another time a complete idea, totally new and original, which I try to impress upon my memory. How did this come to me? A mystery..."

Tchaikovsky with Bob Davidov, his favorite nephew, circa 1891 when Bob was about twenty, two years before the composer's death. He would dedicate the sixth and last symphony (also known as the "Pathétique") to him.

In the spring of 1891 Tchaikovsky was invited to conduct six concerts in the United States. At the top a view of Washington, D.C. in a 19th–century print.

On April 18, 1891 Tchaikovsky boarded ship in Le Havre on the *Bretagne*, heading for the United States and a concert tour. Before leaving he had accepted two commissions from the director of the Imperial Theaters. The first was the opera, *Iolanthe*, for which he had selected a play by a Danish playwright, which in turn was based on a fairy tale by Hans Christian Andersen. The second was a ballet, *The Nutcracker*, based on the well–known story by the German writer E.T.A. Hoffman.

The first concert in the United States took place in the newly completed Carnegie Hall in New York City. The only music by Tchaikovsky on the program was his Royal March. *Because of the short rehearsal time, the only other piece of his played on this tour was his popular* First Piano Concerto.

Just before his departure for the U.S. Tchaikovsky read the sad news in the paper that his sister Alexandra had passed away. He was afraid of the crossing, which indeed turned out to be quite rough. During the month–long tour that followed he did calm down and manage to enjoy, curious traveler he had always been, the visits to New York, Baltimore, Washington D.C., Niagara Falls, and all the new things that cropped up in front of the European traveler. He conducted six concerts and attended a performance of his *Trio in A minor, Opus* 50 at the Russian Embassy. A satisfied man, he returned home to go back to work.

Iolanthe is Tchaikovsky's last opera. The libretto was written by his brother Modest. The hour and a half one–acter was meant to be performed together with *The Nutcracker*, which indeed took place on December 18, 1892. The short, not very dramatic story with a happy ending, takes place in fifteenth– century Provence at the court of King René. His daughter Iolanthe is blind, but lives in such a way she is not aware of the fact. She meets the knight Vodemon in the garden who falls in love with her and tells her the truth. The king sentences him to death, but Iolanthe has fallen in love with him too, and she dearly wants to learn how to see. Owing to her desire and the help of a great Arabian doctor her sight is restored. The opera ends with a marriage.

Besides the opera and the ballet, Tchaikovsky also composed a symphonic poem in this period called *The Voyevode* (not to be confused with the 1867 opera of the same name) using a text by Pushkin as its starting point. Even though it was received warmly by the audience on its inaugural performance in November 1892, the musicians and critics disliked it. Tchaikovsky destroyed the score, but because the arrange-

Top left: *The title page of the orchestral suite from* The Nutcracker. Top right: *The title page to* Iolanthe *(Milan, Library of the Verdi Conservatory).*

Varvara Nikitina and Pavel Gerdt at the première of The Nutcracker *on December 18, 1892.*

ments for orchestra survived the work was later able to be reconstructed.

After the premières of *Iolanthe* and *The Nutcracker* Tchaikovsky embarked on a series of long trips through Europe, and also attended a number of performances of his own music. He even went to the village of Montbéliard where, after many years, he was reunited with his beloved governess Fanny Dürbach. He was to remark: "I thought I was back in Votkinsk and could hear the sound of my mother's voice."

In June 1893 he received an honorary doctorate from Cambridge. Together with Max Bruch, Arrigo Boito, Camille Saint–Saëns, and Edvard Grieg he was made a "Doctor Musicae." One of Nadezhda von Meck's daughters wrote: "The festivities commenced on June 12th. An overture was played by each one of the new doctors. For Tchaikovsky they had chosen *Francesca da*

Rimini. The professors, the lords, and the Maharajah congratulated him, and afterward there was a huge lunch where eulogies were held and exuberant toasts were proclaimed. The following day our doctors wore wide, red robes edged in white silk, and their heads, temporarily devoid of music but replete with amazement, bore velvet berets studded with golden orna-

Tchaikovsky receiving his honorary doctorate in Cambridge, June 1893.

ments. Thus clad, they paraded through the city under a tropical sun, preceded by the Maharajah wearing a golden turban and decked with jewels, and were cheered by an enthusiastic multitude. Tchaikovsky was no longer bored after having made the acquaintance of a Cambridge professor, and he listened on stage to a speech in Latin, and then received his degree. After a garden party and a lunch in London he was allowed to go home."

Left: *The title page of the Sixth Symphony (Milan, Library of the Verdi Museum). Its nickname, "Pathétique" was coined by Tchaikovsky's brother Modest, a few days before its reasonably successful first performance in St. Petersburg on October 28, 1893.*

Right: *Handwritten mss. of the Sixth Symphony. About his last large–scale work, Tchaikovsky wrote to his nephew Bob: "In all sincerity I can say that this symphony is the best thing I have ever written. At any rate, the most sincere. And I love it like I have loved no other score of mine."*

Of all his symphonies, Tchaikovsky's *Sixth Symphony*, which he loved "like no other score I've ever written before," most closely embraced the new ideas concerning symphonic music prevalent in turn–of–the–century Europe, no longer aligned with the classic approach of a Brahms or Dvorák. Rather, Tchaikovsky now showed himself an ally of Bruckner and Mahler, because he too had transgressed the boundaries of the tightly structured traditional symphony so that the symphonic poem arose.

Modest Tchaikovsky, the composer's favorite brother, came up with the name "Pathétique" for the symphony a few days before the première on October 28, 1893 in St. Petersburg. Many biographies on Tchaikovsky state that a few days after the première, he contracted cholera and died. Modest wrote about his death: "His eyes suddenly opened wide. A lucid, fearsome consciousness gleamed from his gaze, which then fixed itself on all of us, then looked up to heaven. For a moment a small light danced in the deepest recesses of his pupils and then he breathed his last. It was shortly after three o'clock in the morning".

The only thing true about this account is probably the time of death. The rest of the events still remain shrouded in mystery, though it seems a small circle of people knew what really happened. The order of events is known: on October 28th the *Sixth Symphony* had its première, on November 3rd it was made known the composer was ill (diagnosed by doctors Lev and Vasily Bertenson), and on November 6th he died. That day, or next a requiem was held for him instigated by the School of Jurisprudence and former

Tchaikovsky's tomb in the ceme-
tery at the Alexander Nevsky
Cloister in St. Petersburg. The
graves of Glinka, Borodin, and
Moussorgsky are nearby.

students of his. On November 8th Dr. Lev Bertenson felt it necessary to publish a detailed account of his patient's illness, and on the thirteenth of the month, at Bertenson's insistence, Modest made public the account of his brother's passing. It would seem both accounts used truth with reckless abandon.

Twelve days after Tchaikovsky's death a memorial concert was held in St. Petersburg on November 18, 1893 by the Russian Music Federation's symphony orchestra, conducted by Eduard Nàpravnik (1839–1915). The performance of the Sixth Symphony, *so shortly after his death made it instantly world famous. It remains one of his most performed masterpieces to this day.*

Left: *Tchaikovsky's writing table in the Tchaikovsky Museum in Klin. He left most of his possessions to his faithful servant Alexei Sofronov, who was able to buy the house in Klin, and fill it with memorabilia of his employer. He sold it four years later to Tchaikovsky's brother Modest and their nephew Bob Davidov. Both would die there, Bob in 1906 of suicide at age thirty–five and Modest, ten years later of cancer. Tchaikovsky's brother Ippolit spent the last years of his life there as its curator, until his death in 1927.*

Right: *Tchaikovsky's workroom in the museum in Klin. Despite serious damage caused by the German invasion in 1941 the room has remained for a large part in its original state.*

ЩЕЛКУНЧИКЪ

Балетъ-Фээрія

въ 2хъ дѣйствіяхъ.

МУЗЫКА

П. ЧАЙКОВСКАГО.

Ор.71.

Оркестровая Партитура	(полная)	150 Руб.
Увертюра Партитура		2 »
Голоса		2 »
Изданіе для Фортепіано	(С.ТАНѢЕВЪ).	5 »
	облегченное авторомъ	4 »

Собственность издателя.

Москва у П. Юргенсона.

С.-Петербургъ у I. Юргенсона. | Варшава у Г. Зенневальда.

Рига у В. Гольца и К°.

Парижъ у Ф. Макаръ и Ноёль. | Лейпцигъ у Д. Ратера.

Rumors were rife in St. Petersburg for years, and the truth began to leak out when Vasily Bertenson finally told the musicologist Georgy Orlov that Tchaikovsky had really taken poison. This account was confirmed by a certain Zander, son of Bertenson's assistant, and by Professor Alexander Ossovsky, who used to work for the Ministry of Justice, where they had already been aware of the fact. Final proof was brought to light by Alexandra Orlova, the above–mentioned musicologist's wife, responsible for digging up all these new facts, when she reported a statement made by Alexander Voitov, a former student at the School of Jurisprudence. He stated: "In 1913, while attending my final year at school, the twentieth anniversary of Tchaikovsky's death was being commemorated. It was then Mrs. Jacobi, the widow of a senior civil servant who had died in 1902, deeply moved as she was by the commemoration, told me the story in the strictest of confidence, that had been torturing her for years. She said that she had decided to confess everything to me because she was old and had no right to take with her to the grave such an important and terrible secret. She told me the following tale. The incident took place in the fall of 1893. Tchaikovsky was in an extremely unfortunate position. Duke Stenbok–Fermor was annoyed at the attention Tchaikovsky had been paying his nephew, and he wrote a letter of complaint to Jacobi to send on to the Czar. As a result of the accusations Tchaikovsky was threatened with the loss of his civil rights, and banishment to Siberia which would lead to his inevitable ruin. It seems both the school and Tchaikovsky's former fellow students had a nasty role in the affair. The school's honor was sacrosanct, and to avoid publicity Jacobi decided on the following: he formed a Council of Honor on which he himself sat. Mrs. Jacobi was in the room where she always was, near her husband's study. Every once and a while she heard voices, sometimes hoarse and excited, at other times whispering. In all it went on for over five hours. Tchaikovsky finally emerged from the study. He seemed uncertain, stumbled, and left without saying a word. He looked pale and on the verge of breaking down. The others in the study kept talking calmly among themselves. When they had gone Jacobi told his wife, swearing her to secrecy, what the council had decided to do with Stenbok–Fermor's letter to the Czar...The former fellow students had come to the conclusion that Tchaikovsky would carry out what he promised to do. They had asked him to commit suicide... The next day news of the composer's lethal illness was spread around St. Petersburg."

According to this controversial theory, Tchaikovsky was therefore the victim of a self–inflicted execution. He was probably given the poison on October 31st by his former fellow student, Auguste Gerke. For two days and nights the composer led an apparently normal life at his brother Modest's house in St. Petersburg. On November 2nd he took the poison during the afternoon meal. He refused to let a doctor come and by the time the Bertensons had arrived the poison had already done its work.

It is far from certain that this is the true account of the events. Other theories are still being put forward, such as that in a fit of depression Tchaikovsky drank water he knew might be infected with cholera. The mystery will probably never be solved. Whatever the case, the most sincere comment on Tchaikovsky came from the Czar, who remarked, "We have got plenty of dukes and barons, but we only have one Tchaikovsky."

Title page to the ballet score of The Nutcracker, *published by the Moscow music publisher, Jurgenson.*

The Most Important Works of Tchaikovsky

Pieces for Orchestra
Romeo and Juliet Overture

1812 Overture

Francesca da Rimini Overture

March Slav

Capriccio Italien

Serenade for Strings

The Tempest

Hamlet Overture

Manfred, symphonic poem

Mozartiana

Symphonies
No. 1 in G minor, "Winter Dreams"

No. 2 in C minor, "The Little Russian"

No. 3 in D major, "Polish"

No. 4 in F minor

No. 5 in E minor

No. 6 in B minor, "Pathétique"

Operas	*The Voyevode*
	The Opritchnik
	Vakula the Blacksmith
	Eugene Onegin
	The Maid of Orleans
	Mazeppa
	The Sorceress
	The Queen of Spades (Pique–Dame)
	Iolanthe
Ballet Music	*Swan Lake*
	The Sleeping Beauty
	The Nutcracker
Concertos	*For piano, no. 1 in B–flat minor*
	For violin, in D major
	Rococo Variations for cello and orchestra
Chamber Music	*Trio for piano in A minor*
	String Sextet, "Souvenirs de Florence"
	String Quartets